Halloween Crafts

Halloween Crafts

35 spooky projects
to make and bake

CICO BOOKS

LONDON NEW YORK

Published in 2013 by CICO Books
An imprint of Ryland Peters & Small Ltd
20–21 Jockey's Fields   519 Broadway, 5th Floor
London WC1R 4BW   New York, NY 10012
www.rylandpeters.com

10 9 8 7 6 5 4 3 2 1

A CIP catalog record for this book is available from the Library
of Congress and the British Library.

ISBN: 978 1 78249 033 3

Printed in China

EDITOR: Clare Sayer
DESIGNER: Louise Turpin

 For digital editions, vistit
www.cicobooks.com/apps.php

NOTE

Standard level spoon measurements are used in all recipes,
unless otherwise stated:
1 tablespoon = one 15ml spoon
1 teaspoon = one 5ml spoon
Both imperial and metric measurements have been given.
Use one set of measurements only and not a mixture of both.
Eggs should be extra large (large) unless otherwise stated.
Butter used in this book is unsalted, unless otherwise stated.
This book contains recipes made with raw eggs. It is prudent for more
vulnerable people, such as pregnant and nursing mothers, babies and
young children, invalids and the elderly, to avoid uncooked dishes made
with eggs. Some of the recipes also contain nuts and should not be
consumed by anyone with a nut allergy.

CONTENTS

INTRODUCTION

THE NIGHTS ARE DRAWING IN, the leaves are turning brown, and the days are getting cooler—summer is definitely over and the Halloween holiday is nearly here! Celebrate the arrival of Fall in style by making your Halloween party one to remember.

With over 35 spooky, creepy, and scary projects there is plenty here to inspire you. There are simple sewing projects, Halloween papercrafts and plenty of spooky baking ideas, all suitable for the beginner crafter or baker. Spooky Decorations has ideas for decorating your house inside and out, from carved pumpkins, table decorations, and balloon ghosts to Halloween bunting and even a scary spider piñata.

Halloween is traditionally all about dressing up and Creepy Costumes has plenty of ideas for your little horrors, from witches and wizards to Frankenstein's monster and a scary skeleton, as well as some great ideas for trick-or-treating bags and buckets. Finally, Scarily Sweet Treats has recipes and ideas for some truly ghoulish party food, from zombie hand cupcakes to spooky cookies and candy apples.

The projects include lists of all materials needed as well as step-by-step instructions, photographs and illustrations, making them easy to follow. Basic techniques are included at the back of the book, and full-size templates are given for all of the costumes.

So, whether you want to decorate your house, be the best dressed kid on the block or wow your friends with some original party food, it's time to get Halloween crafting!

SPOOKY DECORATIONS

Whether you are throwing a party or just staying home waiting for the trick-or-treaters, making Halloween decorations can be great fun. Using scraps of fabric and paper and just a few simple materials you can transform your home into a Halloween house of horror. Carved pumpkins are really effective and easy to do—or why not greet your visitors with a few balloon ghosts?

bat ornaments

These bats would be a cute addition to your Halloween decorating. Just make one, or make a whole cloud of bats to hang all over the house. For extra spookiness, use white thread to add fangs and transform them into vampire bats! The wings need to be quite stiff, so use 100-percent wool felt, or thicker craft felt, or cut an extra layer or two if you're using thin felt.

YOU WILL NEED

* ★ Templates on page 119
* ★ Scissors, pins, needles
* ★ Black felt, approximately 6 x 7in. (15 x 18cm) for each bat
* ★ Dark-gray felt, approximately 3½ x 4¾in. (9 x 12cm) for each bat
* ★ Small pieces of light gray felt
* ★ Matching sewing threads
* ★ Black stranded embroidery floss (thread)
* ★ Two black seed beads, size 8/0 for each bat
* ★ Narrow black ribbon, 6in. (15cm) for each bat

1 Use the templates to cut out two black wing shapes, two dark-gray body shapes, and two light-gray ear shapes.

2 Pin the two wing pieces together. Cut a length of black embroidery floss and set aside half the strands (so for six-stranded floss, use three strands). Using the floss and a large needle, sew the wings together with running stitch, turning the wings over and back again as you sew to ensure the line is neat and straight on both sides. Sew the four dotted lines across the wings first, sewing along each line and then back again, and so filling in the gaps to create a continuous line of stitching. Then sew around the edge of the wings, finishing neatly on one side (this will be the back of the wings). Sewing black on black can be a bit tricky, so make sure you have good light to work by!

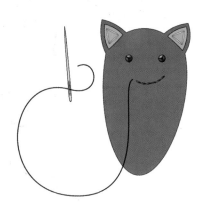

3 Place the two light gray ear shapes on one bat body piece. Sew them in position with a triangle of three stitches in light gray sewing thread. With black sewing thread, sew two black seed beads on as eyes (using three or four stitches per bead) and backstitch a curved smile. If you want to make vampire bats, make a few small stitches with white sewing thread to add two fangs to the smile.

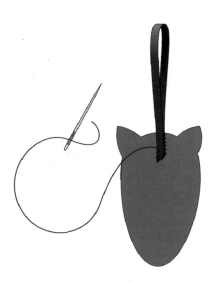

4 Fold the length of narrow black ribbon in half to form a loop and, with ⅜in. (1cm) overlapping the felt, sew the ends to the top of the second bat body shape. Use whip stitches in dark gray sewing thread.

5 Arrange the two bat body shapes on the front and back of the wings (making sure the side of the wings where you finished the stitching is facing backward). Line the body shapes up carefully and pin all three layers together. Sew the layers together by stitching around the edge of the bat body with dark gray sewing thread and small running stitches. Turn the bat over and back again as you sew to ensure a neat line on both sides. Finish the stitches neatly on the back.

ghoulish gravestones

Create a ghoulish graveyard with these fun polystyrene headstones. Write dates, directions, or simply "Boo!" or "Arghhh!", or add personal messages to welcome your guests. Polystyrene insulation board is available from builders' merchants and can usually be bought in quite small pieces—perfect for these gravestones. Rather than buying large pots of paint, try tester pots from your local paint store, which will be much more economical.

YOU WILL NEED

* Polystyrene insulation board
* Serrated bread knife
* Stone-colored gray emulsion paint
* Paintbrush
* Black felt pen
* Craft knife
* Fine paintbrush
* Black emulsion paint
* White paint
* Two 16in. (40cm) dowel rods for each gravestone

1 Cut a piece of polystyrene measuring 24 x 17in. (60 x 43cm) using a bread knife. Draw a curved or rounded top along one short side and cut out carefully, again using the bread knife.

2 Paint the whole board with stone-colored gray paint, dabbing the paintbrush into the cut edges to make sure that they are well covered. Leave to dry.

3 Draw your design onto the gravestone, using the felt pen. With the craft knife, carefully cut out the lettering, numbers or lines, cutting at a slight angle so that it looks like engraving. Remove the cut pieces of polystyrene. You can, of course, omit this cutting stage and simply paint the lettering or numbers directly onto the board, if you like.

4 Paint the letters or numbers and any lines that you have made using the fine paintbrush and some black paint. Do not worry too much about wobbly lines as this will all add to the ancient look of the headstones. If you make any major mistakes, paint over them with the base coat paint. Leave to dry.

5 Mix a little white paint with some of the gray paint to make a light gray color. Put a dry paintbrush into the paint and then dab onto some paper towel to remove the excess paint. The brush should not have too much paint on it—test on some scrap paper, if necessary. Wipe the brush all over the gravestone. Do this roughly and randomly all over the headstone and then leave to dry.

6 Push the two dowel rods into the bottom of the gravestone, about halfway along. Use these rods to push the gravestone into the ground.

Jack-o'-lantern

No Halloween party would be complete without a Jack-o'-lantern. The techniques of cutting away and engraving create different lighting effects—the light pierces, glows, glimmers, and sparkles. See page 50 for a more traditional face, or for a less scary version try the spotted pumpkins on page 22.

YOU WILL NEED

* Water-soluble crayon
* Large, smooth-skinned field pumpkin
* Craft knife
* Kitchen knife
* Large gimlet
* Assorted scooping spoons, including special pumpkin scoop
* Template on page 118
* Dressmaker's pins
* Sharp awl (bradawl)
* Flat-edged woodcarving tool
* Lino-cutting tool
* Glass jar and large, squat, slow-burning candle

1 Mark a crayon circle at the top of the pumpkin, large enough to insert your hand. Cut out first with the craft knife (to make a neat line), then cut deeper with the kitchen knife to cut away. You can pierce the lid with the gimlet to make air holes if you want to use it when the pumpkin is alight.

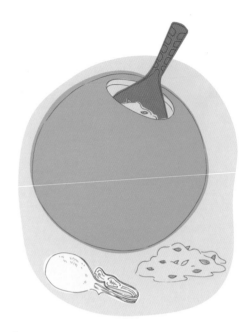

2 Pull out the seeds and flesh, and scoop out the interior using an assortment of spoons (the special pumpkin scoop is ideal for large pumpkins, and an old dessertspoon with the handle bent backward is also useful). Reduce the shell to about ⅜in. (1cm) at the front, but don't worry too much about the back as you will not decorate this part. Tip out all the debris and rinse.

tip

To revive the pumpkin, immerse it in water and keep cool (the fridge is ideal) when not lit. It will last for a number of days if looked after in this way.

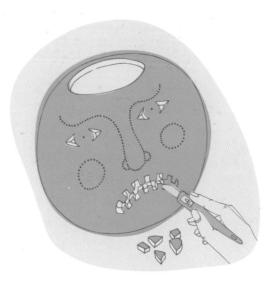

3 Photocopy the template on page 118. Fix in place with dressmakers' pins and prick out the design through the paper onto the skin using the awl. Remove the paper.

4 Refer to your paper template as you begin to carve your design with the woodcarving tool. Carefully cut out the whites of the eyes with the craft knife, taking care to leave the pupil intact. In the same way, cut out the spaces between the teeth.

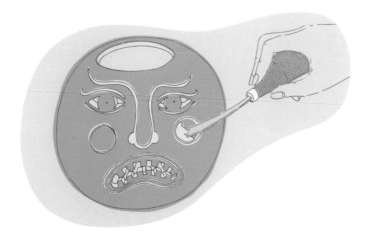

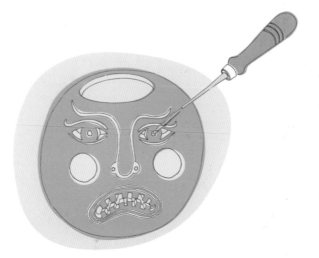

5 Use the lino-cutting tool to engrave the lines around the eyes, eyebrows, and mouth. Make a circle on each cheek and use the woodcarving tool to remove the outer skin. Do the same on the two nostrils.

6 Use the gimlet to carefully drill the hole for the iris in the center of each eye. In the same way, make holes for the nostrils. Insert the glass jar and candle. When lit, you can replace the lid if you wish.

fall wreath

For a more subtle Halloween decoration, make a charming wreath from woolen fabrics in fall colors cut into leaf shapes. I have used eight different fabrics but if you can't get hold of that many then simply increase the sizes of the fabrics that you have and cut more leaves from each one.

YOU WILL NEED

★ Spray adhesive
★ Solid-colored card
★ Eight different tweed and wool fabrics in oranges, browns, and greens, approximately 12 x 12in. (30 x 30cm) each
★ Templates on page 123
★ Scissors
★ Scrap paper
★ Pins
★ Needle and matching sewing thread
★ Craft knife
★ Fast-drying hi-tack PVA glue
★ Polystyrene wreath base, 13¾in. (35cm) in diameter
★ Raffia

1 Working in a well-ventilated area, apply spray adhesive to a piece of colored card and stick the fabric onto it, smoothing it down so that there are no creases or trapped air bubbles. Repeat this for all of the fabric pieces.

2 Using the templates on page 123, cut out three leaf shapes using the scrap paper. Pin and stitch them onto the card-backed fabrics. You will need eight leaves from each fabric, making 64 leaves in total.

3 Cut the leaves out using the scissors. Turn the leaves over so that the card side faces upward and gently score a line along the length of the leaf using the craft knife —make sure that you do not cut in to it. Fold each leaf along the score line to make it more 3D.

4 Glue the leaves onto the wreath base, varying the angles of them and overlapping them so that none of the polystyrene can be seen. Continue sticking the leaves onto the wreath until the whole base is covered.

5 Take a few strands of raffia and tie them into a bow. Glue this onto the wreath. Tie a couple of strands of raffia around the top of the wreath, tying a knot in them to form a loop to hang the wreath in place.

spotty pumpkins

YOU WILL NEED

* ★ Pencil
* ★ Pumpkins
* ★ Thin-bladed knife
* ★ Small spoon
* ★ Apple corer
* ★ Awl (bradawl)
* ★ Votives (tea lights)

Carved Jack-o'-Lanterns are an essential part of Halloween but for a more stylish look, why not make these charming spotty pumpkins? Using an apple corer and an awl, make a dotty decoration on hollowed-out pumpkins, either with a random pattern or in more formal lines or stripes. Never leave lit candles unattended and keep your eye on the pumpkins to make sure that they do not burn.

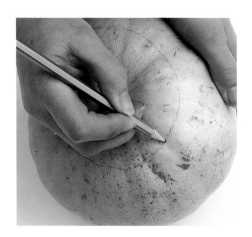

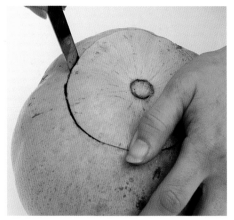

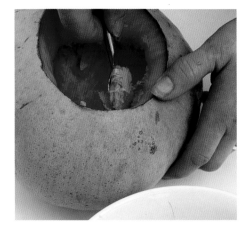

1 Using a pencil, draw a line around the top of the pumpkin about 1½in. (4cm) from the stalk.

2 Take the knife and carefully cut off the top, following the pencil line, to make a lid for the pumpkin. You may need to gently lever the lid off if the seeds and fibers are attached to the lid.

3 Using a strong, small spoon, scoop out the seeds. When the seeds have all been removed, scrape the flesh out of the pumpkin so that the wall of the pumpkin is no more than about ¾in. (2cm) thick. Ensure that you do not make it too thin or you may pierce the skin.

4 Push the apple corer through the flesh to make a hole in the pumpkin. Press the corer firmly onto the skin and twist it slightly to push it in. Make holes randomly all around the pumpkin or in regular lines, if you prefer. Use the awl (bradawl) to make small holes—again randomly or in lines to make a neat pattern.

5 Make holes in the lid with the apple corer, holding the lid carefully so that you do not push the corer into your hand! Put a votive (tea light) inside the pumpkin, light it with a taper or long match and place the lid back on.

pumpkin party bags

Give your guests a party bag with a difference with this gathered fabric and ribbon pumpkin, filled with candies (sweets). Choose orange fabrics in different shades and patterns, using up scraps that you already have, or visit your local fabric store to put together a range of different designs.

YOU WILL NEED

* Squares of orange fabric, about 12 x 12in. (30 x 30cm)
* Plate measuring about 10in. (25cm) in diameter
* Pen
* Scissors
* Candies (sweets)
* 17in. (43cm) wired green ribbon, ⅝in. (1.5cm) wide

1 Press the fabrics so that they are nice and smooth. Lay the plate on the wrong side of a fabric square and draw round it using the pen. Cut the circle out neatly.

2 Put a couple of handfuls of candies (sweets) in the middle of the fabric circle. You may need to add a few more candies or take some away, depending on what type you are using.

3 Gather up the edge of the fabric circle to form a bundle, making sure that the gathers are nicely arranged and that the candies are contained.

4 Hold the gathered top with one hand and tie the ribbon round it with a tight knot, leaving one end of the ribbon at least 4in. (10cm) long. You may find it easier to ask another pair of hands to help on this part! Bind the longer end of the ribbon round the gathered top to form a stalk. Two or three winds of the ribbon should be enough to cover it. Pull it tightly so that it will stay in place.

5 Tie the two ends of ribbon together with a secure knot. Fold the ribbon in half lengthwise to make it narrower. Wind it round a pen, then remove the pen and trim the ends of the ribbon neatly to make a tendril. Repeat with both ends of the ribbon.

fabric bunting

A quick and effective way of decorating large areas ready for Halloween, this fabric bunting is also very cost-efficient. Choose fabrics in oranges and blacks, or try greens and purples for a more dark and menacing look.

1 Take your first piece of fabric and make a small snip in the fabric, 1in. (2.5cm) from the edge and then rip the fabric to make a long strip. Tear from selvage to selvage rather than vertically along as it will be much easier to rip.

2 Continue to make lots of strips from different fabrics. Iron them and pull any odd pieces of thread off them.

3 Cut the strips into shorter pieces ranging from 20–24in. (50–60cm). You will need about 14 strips per meter to make your bunting.

4 Take a strip of fabric and fold it over to make a loop. Lay it over the ribbon.

5 Pull the ends of the strip through the loop above the ribbon and pull.

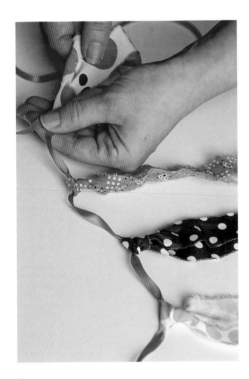

6 Continue to tie the strips, evenly spaced, to the ribbon until you have the desired length. Hang the bunting in place.

balloon ghosts

No Halloween party would be complete without a bunch of visiting ghosts and these balloon spooks couldn't be easier to make. A piece of cheap cotton muslin is hung over a balloon with creepy features made from black card. Tie them in place to decorate a dull corner or fasten them by the front door to welcome trick-or-treaters to your home.

YOU WILL NEED

* ★ White balloon
* ★ White ribbon
* ★ 59in. (150cm) square of white cotton muslin for each ghost
* ★ Scissors
* ★ Approximately 6in. (15cm) square of black card
* ★ Pencil
* ★ Glue

1 Blow the balloon up. Take a length of ribbon making sure that it is long enough for the ghost to be hung up. Tie the ribbon around the balloon knot making sure that it is fastened securely.

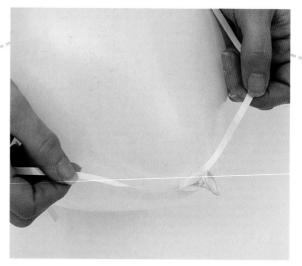

2 Fold the muslin in half and then into quarters. Make a small snip at the folded corner point using the scissors.

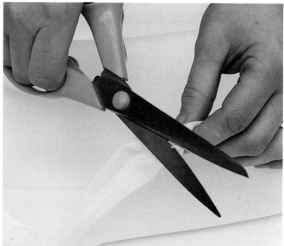

3 Unfold the muslin and thread the ribbon through the hole, pulling the muslin down over the balloon.

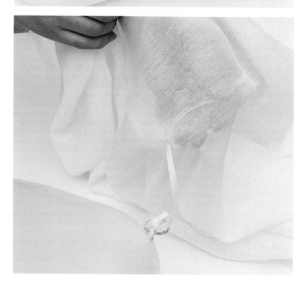

4 Draw two wobbly eyes and a wide, round mouth onto the black card. Cut them out neatly.

5 Stick the eyes and mouth onto the muslin over the balloon using the glue. Make sure that they are well stuck down. Create a collection of ghosts, making the facial features different for each one. Hang the ghosts in place using the ribbon.

spotty hanging decorations

These hanging decorations can be used vertically, as a room divider or mobile decoration, or hung as bunting, across the room in swags. Choose papers that are thin enough to machine stitch, using interesting patterns for added interest. Use a new needle on your sewing machine so that it will stitch through the papers without a problem.

1 Using the compass, draw three circles with the pencil onto scrap card measuring 1⅜in. (3.5cm), 2in. (5cm), and 3¼in. (8cm) in diameter. Cut them out.

YOU WILL NEED

* **Compass**
* **Pencil**
* **Scrap card**
* **Ruler**
* **Scissors**
* **Solid-colored and patterned paper or thin card in oranges, reds, and blacks**
* **Orange sewing thread**
* **Sewing machine**

2 Use your scrap card discs to draw circles onto the solid-colored and patterned papers and thin cards. Place the discs as close together as you can to get as many circles as possible.

3 Settle down comfortably and cut the circles out as neatly as you can. This may take a while!

4 Arrange the circles in a line, making sure that no two circles of the same paper or card are next to each other. For a hanging decoration 63in. (160cm) long you will need approximately six large circles, nine medium circles and ten small circles.

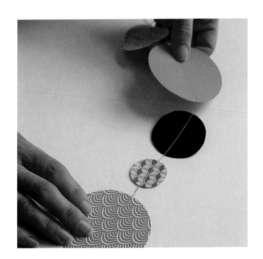

5 Pull about 16in. (40cm) of thread from the sewing machine to hang the decoration with and begin to stitch the circles together leaving a gap of about ³⁄₈in. (1cm) between each one. Trim the thread neatly on the bottom circle and hang up.

cobweb table decoration

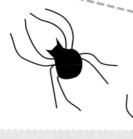

For a really quick, easy, and inexpensive Halloween decoration, simply cut up and rip a piece of white cotton muslin to make a cobwebby table-covering to really set the scene. Making the cloth in situ makes it easier to see what you are doing, and laying the muslin over some black fabric makes it really stand out. For extra decoration, simply tear strips of muslin about 1½in. (4cm) wide and drape them over candelabras—making sure that the muslin is a safe distance away from any lit candles. Adding a few pieces of ivy will really finish the look.

YOU WILL NEED

★ Black fabric to cover the table
★ Length of cotton muslin, enough to cover your table
★ Sharp fabric scissors

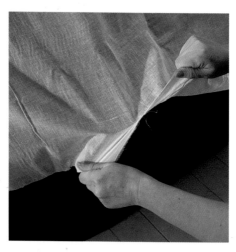

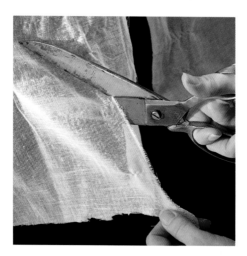

1 Lay the black fabric onto the table. Cut away the selvage from both edges of the muslin. Place it over the top of the black fabric so that it reaches about halfway down the table. Cut a small snip in the edge of the muslin.

2 Take hold of the muslin either side of the snip you have just made and pull to tear the muslin.

3 Make a cut into the tear at an angle. As it is not easy to rip at an angle, use scissors and pull the threads along the cut edge a little to make it look more ragged.

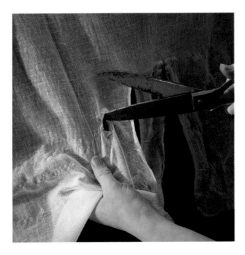

4 Now make a hole in the muslin, again with the scissors, cutting it roughly.

5 Tear the muslin around the hole, making the edges look rough. Continue to cut and tear the muslin all the way round randomly from the bottom up and make holes in it to make your cobweb cloth.

spider piñata

YOU WILL NEED

- ★ Two large balloons
- ★ Masking tape
- ★ Newspaper
- ★ PVA glue
- ★ Bowl
- ★ Black yarn
- ★ Eight thick black pipe cleaners
- ★ Pin
- ★ Craft knife
- ★ Candies (sweets) and little gifts
- ★ Small paintbrush
- ★ Black tissue paper
- ★ Purple tissue paper
- ★ Two small colored buttons
- ★ Two white buttons

FOR THE STICK

- ★ 24in. (60cm) wooden baton, 1¼in. (3cm) wide
- ★ PVA glue
- ★ 78in. (200cm) each of black, orange, and purple ribbon, ⅝in. (1.5cm) wide

This fun papier-mâché spider piñata is sure to go down well at your Halloween party. Use two balloons to form the mold for the paper mache, and decorate with strips of tissue paper to make a delightfully hairy spider. Add candies (sweets) and small gifts (making sure that you do not use anything too heavy), and make a bright, colorful stick using ribbons to hit the piñata with.

1 Blow the balloons up, making one larger than the other and tie at the top. Place them together with the knots next to each other and use the masking tape to tape them together to form the spider's shape—a head and a slightly larger body.

2 Tear the newspaper into pieces about 4 x 2½in. (10 x 6cm). Make a thin glue in a bowl using one part PVA glue to one part water. Dip the paper pieces into the glue and smooth onto the balloons. Cover both balloons, overlapping the pieces of paper so that the balloons cannot be seen at all. Leave to dry. Repeat twice to make three layers in total.

3 Cut a length of black yarn long enough to hang the piñata from and tape one end to the body balloon and one end to the head balloon. Stick more papier-mâché pieces over the ends of the yarn to hold them securely in place.

4 Tape four pipe cleaner legs onto each side of the body. Again, papier-mâché over the ends of the pipe cleaners and tape to hold them in place.

5 Stick a pin through both the body and the head to pop the balloons. Draw a flap (three sides of a square) onto the top of the body and cut it neatly with a craft knife. Put your hand into the body and remove the bits of balloon. Put candies and small gifts inside the body and papier-mâché over the flap to seal it again.

6 Cut squares of black tissue paper, about 3in. (8cm) square. Papier-mâché these all over the spider, placing the tissue paper neatly around the legs and the wool hanging at the top. Leave to dry completely.

7 Cut strips of black tissue paper about 2½in. (6cm) wide and cut small snips about 1½in. (4cm) long all the way along it about ⅜in. (1cm) apart. Using the paintbrush, paste some glue in a circle at the end of the bigger part of the body. Glue a strip of cut tissue paper onto it, cutting it to the right length. Apply more glue on another ring around this and glue another strip of cut tissue paper onto it.

8 Continue to glue the black tissue paper around the body and then cut a few strips of purple tissue paper in the same way. Glue two strips of purple tissue paper and then continue with the black.

9 When the whole spider is covered in tissue paper strips, glue the smaller colored buttons onto the center of the white buttons and then glue them onto the face of the spider.

10 To make a stick to hit the piñata, take the wooden baton and glue the end of the black ribbon to the end of the baton. Wrap the ribbon around the stick leaving a gap about the width or two ribbons between each wrap. When you get to the end of the baton glue the ribbon to the end securely, leaving the rest of the ribbon loose.

11 Glue the end of your orange ribbon to the end of the baton and again wrap the orange ribbon around the baton just above the black ribbon.

12 Glue the orange ribbon to the end of the stick securely as before, leaving the rest of the ribbon loose. Repeat this using purple ribbon and glue in place as before.

haunted house lanterns

Create a glow with a row of little haunted house lanterns. Make the houses from gray cardboard, adding wonky windows and wooden bars to make them look suitably rickety. Use battery-operated votives (tea lights) inside the lanterns, keeping lit candles well away.

YOU WILL NEED

* Templates on page 120-122
* Pencil
* Scissors
* 16 x 10in. (40 x 26cm) gray cardboard for each house
* Craft knife and cutting mat
* Metal ruler (optional)
* 8in. (20cm) square thin black card for each house
* Glue stick
* Orange tissue paper
* Wooden popsicle (lolly) sticks
* Rotary hole punch
* Battery operated-votives (tea lights)

1 Use the templates on page 120-121 to draw and cut out the basic shapes for the front and back of the house from gray cardboard, cutting out the windows and doors where indicated. Follow the lines indicated to make the smaller house. Use the craft knife and cutting mat to make clean, neat cuts, using a metal ruler, if you find it helpful.

2 Use the templates on page 122 to cut out windows and a door from black card, again using the craft knife and cutting mat, with a metal ruler if necessary.

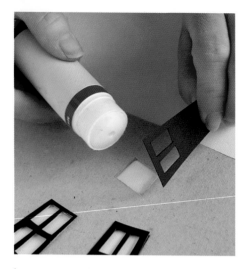

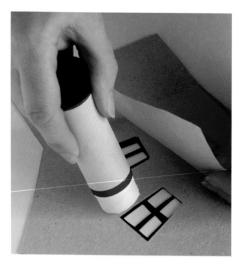

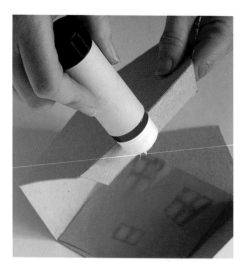

3 Stick the black windows and door over the holes cut in the house using the glue stick. Press them down to make sure that they are well adhered.

4 Cut a piece of orange tissue paper 4 x 4½in. (10 x 11.5cm) and glue onto the back of the windows and door using the glue stick. If making the smaller house, cut a piece that is 4x4in. (10x10cm).

5 Use the craft knife and cutting mat to score along the fold lines on the inside of the house—making sure that you do not cut into the card too much. Fold along the score lines and apply glue along the flap you have created. Stick the house together.

6 Use the templates on page 121 to cut short strips of black card and glue them to the front of the house to create a rickety fence. Cut two pieces of popsicle (lolly) stick about 1½in. (4cm) long and glue them across a window or a door. Draw tiny nails onto both ends of the popsicle sticks. Using the templates on page 121 cut out bats and spiders from black card and glue them onto the front of the house.

7 Using the templates on page 122, cut out a roof, choosing either to leave it plain or to cut a scalloped or jagged edge. Punch holes along the scalloped edge with the hole punch.

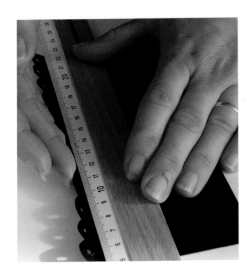

8 Score the edge of the roof along the fold lines using the craft knife and fold along the score lines.

9 Cut out a chimney using the template on page 121, fold along the line and glue onto the roof. Place the battery operated votive (tea light) inside the house and put the roof on top.

fiendishly frightening tablecloth

YOU WILL NEED

* Scissors, pins, and needles
* 4½ x 55in. (11.5 x 140cm) purple gingham fabric
* 47¼ x 55in. (120 x 140cm) natural linen fabric
* 4⅛ x 55in. (10.5 x 140cm) black polka dot fabric
* 3¾ x 55in. (9.5 x 140cm) black and white gingham fabric
* 55in. (140cm) black rick rack trim
* Black sewing thread
* Approximately 40 black buttons in various sizes
* Four 1¼in. (3cm) black buttons
* Black embroidery floss (thread)
* Embroidery needle

This spidery tablecloth will form a centerpiece to your Halloween decorations that is smart as well as spooky. Collect odd buttons to decorate it with, gluing them in place if you are short of time, and add spiders' legs with a few simple embroidery stitches. The finished tablecloth is 53½ x 55¾in. (136 x 141.4cm). All seam allowances are ⅜in. (1cm.)

1 Pin the purple gingham fabric to the main linen fabric along the long edge, right sides together. Machine stitch them together and press the seam open.

2 Take the polka-dot fabric and pin it to the purple gingham fabric in the same way, right sides together. Machine stitch all the way down and then press the seam open.

3 Pin the black and white gingham fabric to the polka-dot fabric in the same way and machine stitch in place. Press the seam open as before.

4 Pin the rick-rack to the right side of the tablecloth, along the join where the purple gingham meets the main linen fabric. Machine stitch in place, using black sewing thread.

halloween rosette decorations

YOU WILL NEED

★ Tissue paper in black and shades of orange
★ Ruler
★ Pencil
★ Scissors
★ Clear thread
★ Scalloped-edge scissors
★ Glue stick
★ Compass
★ Scrap card
★ Patterned papers and card

These striking tissue paper rosettes will add a touch of style to your decorations. Hang them on a wall to create a bold display or stick them up at a window so that they will be seen from inside and out. Make a central circular card decoration for both sides of the rosette if they are to be hung at a window so that they will look good from both sides.

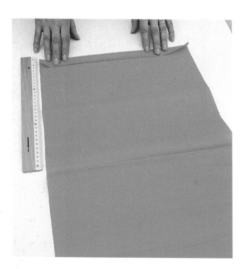

1 Measure and cut a rectangle of tissue paper 27¼ x 13¾in. (70 x 35cm) using the ruler, pencil, and scissors. Make a fold along one short edge 1in. (2.5cm) deep. Press along the fold to make a neat edge.

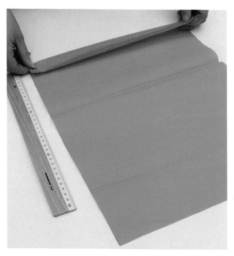

2 Turn the tissue paper over and fold over again by the same depth. Turn the paper over again and continue folding the paper in a concertina until you get to the end.

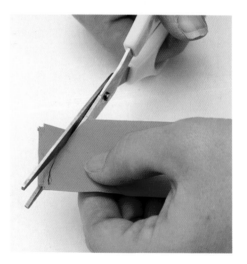

3 Make a snip at one end of the paper to make a small point, cutting from on the top of one edge diagonally down to about ¾in. (2cm). Repeat at the other end. Try cutting a curve or a point on some of the rosettes for a more frilly edging.

4 Cut a piece of clear thread 40in. (100cm) long (or longer if they are to be hung in a tall room). Fold the tissue paper strip in half, matching the pointed ends and crease along the fold. Tie the thread around the tissue paper and secure with a knot.

5 Apply glue along one side of the tissue paper strip and press the thread along it. Fold the tissue paper over to stick the two sides together.

6 Glue along one of the other sides of the tissue paper and stick together, opening up the rosette as you do it.

7 Draw four circles onto scrap card using the compass, the largest with a diameter of 6in. (15cm), the next 4¾in. (12cm), one measuring 3¼in. (8cm), and the smallest 1¼in. (4cm). Cut them out with the scalloped-edge scissors.

8 Use these card circles to make circles of colored and patterned paper and card, and cut them out. Stick them together, arranging the colors and patterns so that they are all different.

9 Glue the back of the discs and stick them onto the tissue paper rosettes. If the rosettes are to hang in the middle of the room, then stick a decorative disc on both sides of the rosette.

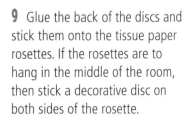

grinning **pumpkin**

Let your creativity loose with this carved pumpkin with its spooky grin. Use the templates provided or draw your own face, adding eyebrows and a toothy grin for a truly creepy look. It is possible to buy pumpkin carving tools from craft stores and online companies, but if these are not available simply use a thin-bladed knife and work slowly and carefully around the curved lines.

YOU WILL NEED

* ★ Pencil
* ★ Pumpkin
* ★ Thin-bladed knife
* ★ Small, strong spoon
* ★ Template on page 118
* ★ Scrap paper
* ★ Scissors
* ★ Votive (tea light)

1 Using a pencil, draw a jagged line around the top of the pumpkin, making it the same distance from the stalk all the way round.

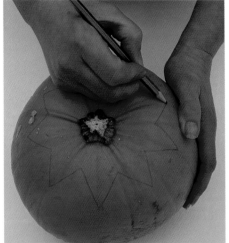

2 Take the knife and cut through the pencil line on the pumpkin. Carefully cut along all of the jagged lines and gently ease off the lid.

tIP

Choose your pumpkin carefully—try to find one that is a good round shape with enough space for you to add all your spooky features!

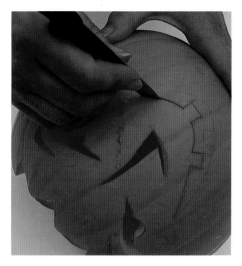

3 Scoop the seeds out of the pumpkin and carefully scrape out the interior using the spoon so that the flesh is about ¾in. (2cm) thick. Make sure that you do not puncture the skin.

4 Using the template on page 118, cut out the features for the face on some scrap paper. Hold them in place, piece by piece, and draw round them with a pencil.

5 Cut through the pencil lines carefully with the knife, slowly and neatly cutting along the curved lines. Remove any of the cut-out pieces of pumpkin and discard.

6 Cut vertical slits around the back of the pumpkin to let more light out of the pumpkin. Make sure that the slits are not too near the bottom of the pumpkin.

7 Put a votive (tea light) inside the pumpkin and light it with a taper or a long match, putting the lid carefully back on the pumpkin.

tIP

Never leave a lit candle or votive (tea light) unattended and remove the lid if it starts to burn.

CREEPY COSTUMES

Let your creativity fly with these fabulous ideas for Halloween costumes! Halloween is all about dressing up and this chapter has plenty of simple ideas for children of all ages, from cute to downright creepy. Choose from a black cat, a spooky spider, or witches and wizards—there's even a scary alien. And once you're done, why not make a trick-or-treat bag to hold all your goodies?

spooky spider

Who says creepy crawly spiders can't be cute? Woolly tights are used for the legs, and a fabric body and helmet with felt antennae complete the look. Try stripy tights for a colorful costume or make the body from fake fur for a really hairy spider.

YOU WILL NEED

* ★ Scissors
* ★ 46 x 26in. (116 x 65cm) fabric for the body and matching thread
* ★ Ruler
* ★ Pins
* ★ 74in. (186cm) black elastic ¼in. (5mm) wide
* ★ Safety pin
* ★ Four pairs of black wool adult tights
* ★ Fiberfill (stuffing)
* ★ 24 x 16in. (60 x 40cm) black felt
* ★ Embroidery floss (thread) and embroidery needle
* ★ 116in. (290cm) black ribbon ¼in. (5mm) wide
* ★ Black cotton jersey fabric and matching thread
* ★ Small patch of Velcro
* ★ Fabric glue
* ★ Black tights or leggings and black long-sleeved top (to complete costume)

1 Cut your main fabric into two rectangles, each 23 x 26in. (58 x 65cm). To mark out the armholes, with a ruler measure 2in. (5cm) down from each top corner on both squares of fabric and cut a snip ¾in. (2cm) long. Measure 8in. (20cm) down from each snip and cut another snip. With right sides together, pin and stitch the two fabric squares together at the sides above and below the top and bottom snips, using ¾in. (2cm) seams. Press the seams open and turn right side out.

2 Turn under the ¾in. (2cm) seam allowances of the armholes. Pin and stitch in place parallel to each armhole opening, and across the top and bottom of each armhole twice, in order to reinforce them. Press.

3 At the top and bottom edges, turn under ¾in. (2cm). Pin and stitch in place to create channels, leaving a small opening for the elastic. Cut two pieces of elastic about 22in. (55cm) long and thread through the top and bottom channels using a safety pin attached to one end of the elastic. Remove the safety pin, sew the ends of each piece of elastic together, and stitch the opening of each channel closed.

4 To make the legs, cut the legs off the tights so that they are about 22in. (55cm) long. Stuff them with fiberfill (stuffing), making sure that there are no lumps and bumps.

5 Using pattern **piece 1**, cut two oval shapes from black felt for the back. Cut two 15in. (38cm) lengths of black elastic and tie the ends of each in a knot. Pin these two loops onto one of the felt pieces in the center, about 5in. (12cm) apart, and machine stitch about 2in. (5cm) of the elastic onto the felt. These elastic loops will loop over your child's arms and hold the costume on.

6 Lay this back piece, elastic-side down, on the work surface and pin four of the legs on top, along one side; stitch. Pin the remaining four legs along the other side of the felt and again machine stitch in place. This can be rather unwieldy, so make sure that you have plenty of space around your sewing machine!

7 Pin the other back piece on top and push fiberfill (stuffing) between the layers to pad it slightly. Using embroidery floss and a needle, sew running stitch all the way around through all the layers.

8 Lay the spider flat on the work surface, with the legs evenly spaced. Hand sew a 22in. (55cm) ribbon to the back of each of the four legs on one side of the spider, sewing it securely near the end of each leg. Turn both ends of the ribbon under and hand sew for a neat finish. Repeat for the other four legs with a second ribbon.

9 Cut two 30in. (75cm) lengths of ribbon and tie one around the top leg on each side of the spider with a firm knot. These will be used to tie the legs to your child's wrists.

10 To make the hat, use pattern **piece 2** to cut two pieces from black jersey. With right sides together, pin and stitch them together along the outward-curving edge with a ⅜in. (1cm) seam.

11 Turn under ⅜in. (1cm) along the raw edges, pin, and machine stitch in place. Turn under the ends of the straps by the same amount and sew the two pieces of a Velcro patch to them, to the underside of one strap and to the top of the other. Turn the hat right side out. Measure and cut two pieces of black felt 3in. (7.5cm) square. Apply glue to one side of each and roll them up, holding them in place until the glue dries. (You can wrap rubber bands around them while they are drying if you wish.) Hand sew them onto the top of the hat, about 2in. (5cm) from the front edge.

wonderful wizard

Alacazam and abracadabra—this outfit will put a spell on any child who sees it. The simple dress pattern is transformed into a striking gown when decorated with spell-binding stars, and a cloak and hat finish the look.

1 Make the satin gown using pattern **pieces 25 and 28** and following the directions for the **Basic Dress on page 117**. Iron fusible web (Bondaweb) onto the back of the silver fabric following the manufacturer's directions. Using pattern **piece 23**, draw stars on the backing paper and cut out enough stars for the gown and hat. Arrange some on the gown and iron them on, again following the manufacturer's directions.

2 Using pattern **piece 3**, cut out a hat shape from posterboard (card) and from satin fabric using the correct lines for each on the pattern. Bend the posterboard shape into a cone and glue the straight edges together, overlapping them by ³⁄₈in. (1cm). Iron stars onto the right side of the fabric hat shape as before. Right sides together, pin and stitch the straight edges together and trim the seam allowance. Turn right side out and slip this over the posterboard hat. Glue the fabric inside the rim of the hat to form a neat bottom edge.

YOU WILL NEED

* 48 x 52in. (115 x 112cm) satin fabric for the gown
* Matching sewing thread
* Needle, scissors, and pins
* 20in. (50cm) square of fusible web (Bondaweb)
* 20in. (50cm) square of silver fabric for the stars
* Posterboard (card)
* Ruler or measuring tape
* 18in. (45cm) elastic ¼in. (5mm) wide
* Safety pin
* 46 x 45in. (115 x 112cm) satin fabric for the cloak and hat
* High-tack craft glue
* 60in. (150cm) silver ribbon 1³⁄₈in. (3.5cm) wide

3 For the cloak, measure and cut a 30 x 45in. (76 x 112cm) rectangle of satin. Press under ⅜in. (1cm) on the two short edges and one long edge, and then press under another ⅜in. (1cm). Pin and stitch. Press under ⅜in. (1cm) on the remaining raw edge and then another ¾in. (2cm). Pin and stitch, forming a channel.

4 For the ties, thread the silver ribbon through the channel using a safety pin. Pull the ribbon through until the neck edge is gathered up and the ends of the ribbon are the same length, for tying in a big bow.

Whether a child wants to be a good or a wicked witch, this costume is ideal for trick-or-treating. Choose net in spooky colors to make the skirt and team it with stripy tights, adding felt buckles glued onto plain sneakers for a perfect Halloween look.

enchanting witch

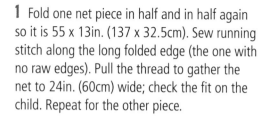

1 Fold one net piece in half and in half again so it is 55 x 13in. (137 x 32.5cm). Sew running stitch along the long folded edge (the one with no raw edges). Pull the thread to gather the net to 24in. (60cm) wide; check the fit on the child. Repeat for the other piece.

2 Pin and baste the two skirts together along the top. Now pin and stitch the wider ribbon along the top. Fold 12in. (30cm) lengths of ribbon in half and sew the folded ends to the ribbon waistband. Cut along the folds at the bottom of the skirt, then cut V-shapes from the net on this edge, cutting each layer separately to make a jagged lower edge.

3 To make the hat, cut out a top and brim from black felt using pattern **pieces 3 and 4**. Fold the top in half, right sides together, matching the long edges. Pin and machine stitch a ⅜in. (1cm) seam down the long edge. Turn right side out.

4 Pin the felt brim to the bottom edge of the hat top. Hand sew all the way around using small, neat overhand stitches. Glue a length of narrow ribbon around the hat to decorate it, overlapping the ends neatly.

YOU WILL NEED

* 52 x 55in. (130 x 137cm) each of black net and purple net for the skirt
* 51in. (127cm) ribbon 1½in. (4cm) wide for the skirt waistband
* 82in. (205cm) ribbon ¼in. (5mm) wide for the skirt
* 22 x 48in. (54 x 120cm) black felt for the hat
* Matching sewing threads
* Pins
* High-tack craft glue
* 30 x 45in. (76 x 112cm) black fabric for the cloak
* 60in. (150cm) velvet ribbon ¾in. (2cm) wide for the cloak
* Scrap of gold felt for buckles on the shoes
* Black sneakers
* Black top and striped leggings, tights, or socks (to complete costume)

tip

To make the cloak, follow the directions for the Wizard's cloak (page 61), altering the length, if necessary. Leave the cloak plain or decorate with star and moon shapes. For the shoes, make two buckles from gold felt and glue them onto sneakers to complete your witchy outfit.

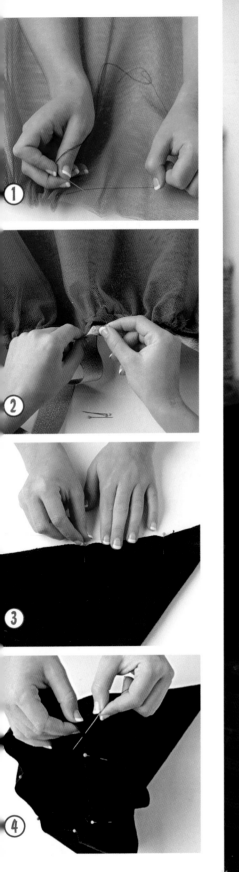

cute jack-o'-lantern

Can you possibly say you have seen a jack-o'-lantern as cute as this one? Choose medium- to heavy-weight fabric so that the lantern will hold its shape, then use the design for the face shown here or design your own to create scary and spooky faces to freak out your friends.

YOU WILL NEED

* 48 x 30in. (120 x 74cm) orange fabric
* Matching sewing thread
* Scrap of black felt
* Pins
* Ruler or measuring tape
* 44in. (110cm) elastic 1/4in. (5mm) wide
* Safety pin
* 28 x 29in. (70 x 72cm) green felt
* Two green jumbo pipe cleaners
* Small patch of Velcro
* Green top, green leggings, and black sneakers (to complete costume)

tIP

Dress your little pumpkin in green leggings and a plain top to finish the outfit. If you can't get hold of store-bought ones, dye a plain white top and leggings with green fabric dye that is suitable for use in the washing machine.

1 Measure and cut out two 23 x 28in. (58 x 70cm) rectangles of orange fabric. Using pattern **pieces 8 and 9**, cut out three triangles and a mouth shape from black felt. Pin and stitch them to the middle of one of the orange fabric pieces. To mark out the armholes, with a ruler measure 2in. (5cm) down from each top corner on both squares of fabric and cut a snip ¾in. (2cm) long. Measure 8in. (20cm) down from each snip and cut another snip. With right sides together, pin and stitch the two fabric squares together at the sides above and below the top and bottom snips, using ¾in. (2cm) seams. Press the seams open. Turn right side out.

2 Turn under the ¾in. (2cm) seam allowances of the armholes. Pin and stitch in place parallel to each armhole opening, and across the top and bottom of each armhole twice, in order to reinforce them. Press.

3 At the top and bottom edges, turn under ¾in. (2cm). Pin and stitch in place to create channels, leaving a small opening for the elastic. Cut two pieces of elastic about 22in. (55cm) long and thread through the top and bottom channels using a safety pin attached to one end of the elastic. Remove the safety pin, sew the ends of each piece of elastic together, and stitch the opening of each channel closed.

4 Using pattern **piece 10**, cut out six hat pieces from green felt. Pin and stitch three together along the sides using ¼in. (5mm) seams. Repeat with the remaining three pieces.

5 Pin and stitch the two halves of the hat together using ¼in. (5mm) seams. Twist the pipe cleaners to look like tendrils and push them through the seam at the top of the hat. Make a few small stitches inside the hat to hold the pipe cleaners in place, and make sure that the ends are bent over so that there are no sharp wires.

6 Using pattern **piece 11**, cut out a collar shape from green felt. It won't be sewn on, so pin and stitch the two pieces of the Velcro patch to the back corners, to the underside of one and to the top of the other.

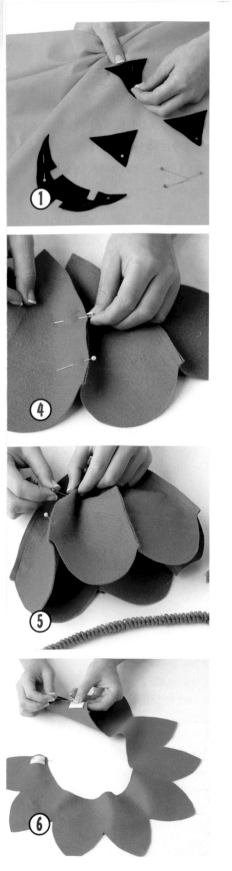

Frankenstein's monster

He's alive! Ten thousand volts of lightning were needed to bring Frankenstein's monster to life, but you will only need a few cardboard boxes, some fabric, and thread. Practice your scariest monster face before you go out trick-or-treating to guarantee your best candy haul ever.

1 Make the top and pants using pattern **pieces 26a, 26b, and 27** and following the directions on **pages 114 and 115**. Cut 4in. (10cm) squares of assorted fabrics using pinking shears, and stitch them randomly onto the top. Using embroidery floss, make large stitches around them for decoration.

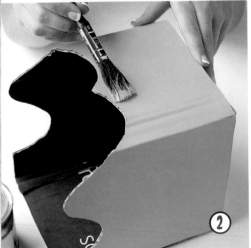

2 Using a craft knife, cut off the top of the box for the head, and turn the box upside down. Cut ear shapes from the sides and a brow from the front. Paint the head green and leave to dry completely.

3 Cut six 6 x ¾in. (15 x 2cm) strips of black felt and glue them onto the top of the head. Cut out two felt eyebrow shapes and glue them onto the face.

YOU WILL NEED

* ★ 45 x 44in. (114 x 110cm) brown fabric for the top
* ★ 49 x 34in. (124 x 85cm) gray fabric for the pants
* ★ Scraps of fabric for patches
* ★ Matching sewing threads
* ★ Pinking shears
* ★ Embroidery floss (thread) and needle
* ★ Craft knife
* ★ Cardboard box approx 6½ x 6½ x 8in. (17 x 17 x 20cm) for the head
* ★ Green and brown water-based paint and paintbrush
* ★ Black felt
* ★ High-tack craft glue
* ★ Black marker pen
* ★ Two bottle tops
* ★ Two cardboard boxes for the shoes approx 9 x 4½ x 3½in. (23 x 11 x 9cm)
* ★ Two 28in. (70cm) pieces of black cord

little red riding hood

This cute red cape is perfect for scaring away any wolves lurking in the woods. The gingham lining really makes the cloak stand out, but for a simpler version, miss out the lining and simply hem all the way round the cape and sew ribbons on for the ties.

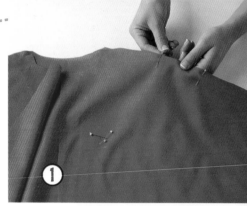

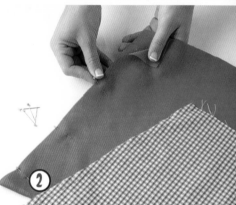

YOU WILL NEED

* ★ Scissors and pins
* ★ 73 x 53in. (185 x 134cm) red fabric
* ★ 73 x 53in. (185 x 134cm) gingham fabric
* ★ Matching sewing threads
* ★ Two 24in. (60cm) lengths of 1in. (2.4cm) wide ribbon
* ★ Jumbo rick-rack

1 For the cape, use pattern **pieces 29** and **30** to cut out one back and two front pieces from red fabric and the same from gingham fabric. With right sides together, pin and machine stitch the red fronts to the red back with ⅜in. (1cm) seams. Press the seams open. Do the same for the gingham pieces.

2 Using pattern **piece 31**, cut out one hood piece from red fabric and one from gingham. Fold the red fabric in half with right sides together, and pin and stitch along the angled edge. Press the seams open. Turn right side out. Repeat for the gingham piece.

3 With right sides together and raw edges lined up, pin and stitch the lower edge of the red hood to the top edge of the red cape. Repeat for the gingham pieces, leaving an opening of about 5in. (12cm) in the seam.

4 Baste (tack) the ends of the ribbons to the right side of the red cape at the neck. Pin and baste the rick-rack on the right side along the ⅜in. (1cm) seamline on the bottom edge of the cape, and along the ⅜in. (1cm) seamline on the raw edge of the hood. With right sides together, pin and stitch the gingham lining to the red cape all the way around with a ⅜in. (1cm) seam. Snip into the seam allowances on the curves. Turn the cape right side out through the opening in the lining. Press. Slipstitch the opening closed.

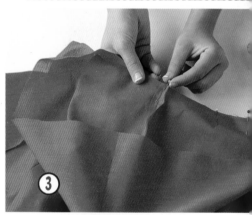

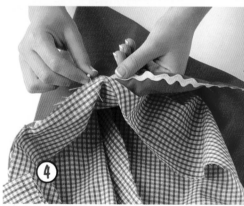

Every trick-or-treater needs a bag to stash their goodies in, and this sweet pumpkin bag is just the job. Felt is easy to use and because it doesn't fray, you won't need to hem it, making it perfect for this project. Raid your button box for green buttons—using different sizes and shades—to finish the look.

pumpkin trick-or-treat bag

YOU WILL NEED

* ★ Templates on page 123
* ★ Scissors
* ★ 18 x 12in. (46 x 30cm) orange felt
* ★ 6 x 6in. (16 x 16cm) green felt
* ★ Pins
* ★ Sewing machine
* ★ Orange and green sewing thread
* ★ Ruler or measuring tape
* ★ About 20 green buttons in different sizes
* ★ Needle
* ★ Pinking shears

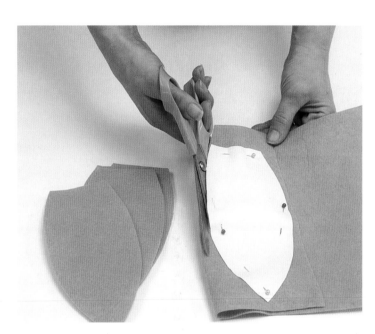

1 Using the template on page 123, cut out six segments from orange felt.

2 Again using the template on page 123, cut out six leaf sections from green felt. Pin a leaf shape to an orange felt segment, lining up the top straight edges. Thread your sewing machine with green thread for the top stitching and orange thread for the under stitching and then machine stitch a leaf to each orange segment. Trim the threads.

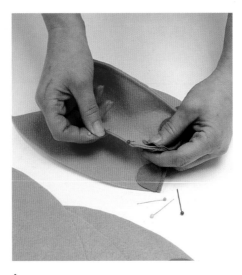

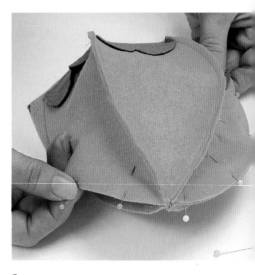

3 With wrong sides together (the right side being the one with the leaf stitched to it), pin and stitch two orange segments together. Trim the threads.

4 Pin and stitch a third orange segment to the one of the orange segments already stitched together in the same way. Repeat this with the remaining three segments to make the two halves of the bucket.

5 Pin and stitch the two halves together to form the bucket. Trim the threads.

6 Measure and cut one strip of orange felt 12 x 1⅜in. (30 x 3.5cm) and two strips of green felt 12 x ¾in. (30 x 2cm). Pin a green strip centrally along the orange strip and machine stitch in place. Trim the threads. Pin and stitch the second green strip to the other side of the orange strip and again machine stitch in place, then trim the threads.

7 Use the pinking shears to cut the orange strip along both sides of the green strips to make a decorative edging along the handle.

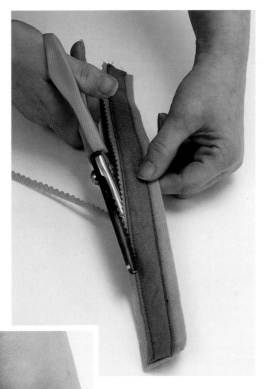

8 Pin and stitch one end of the handle to the inside of the felt bucket, stitching a few times to make the handle strong. Stitch the other end of the handle in place directly opposite the first end, again reinforcing the stitches.

9 Hand stitch a few buttons onto each segment of the bucket to decorate, sewing them on securely so that they will not get knocked off when trick-or-treating.

trick-or-treat bucket

Transform a plain metal bucket into a magnificent Egyptian mummy trick-or-treat bucket, ideal for carrying your candy collection. Strips of muslin are wrapped around the bucket to form the bandages, with two scary, bloodshot eyes peeping through to frighten all who may step into your path. Alternatively, make a black cat or a funny Frankenstein from colored card and buttons, all quick to do—and inexpensive, too.

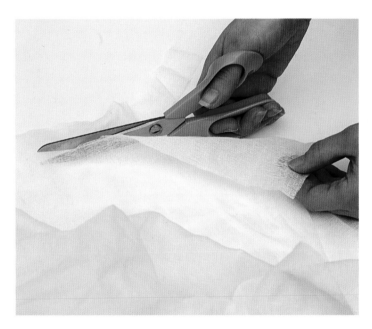

1 Cut a strip of muslin about 1½in. (4cm) wide, cutting from edge to edge. Repeat until you have six strips.

2 Take two of the strips and tie them together at the ends with a knot. Leaving one of the strips aside for now, join all the strips together in this way to make one long strip.

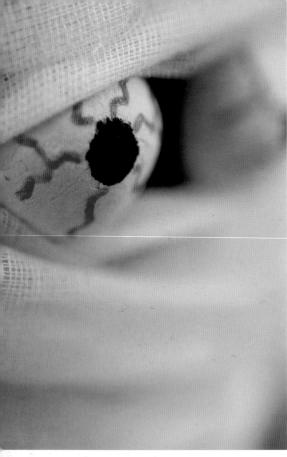

3 Position the piece of black card onto the front of the bucket and sellotape it in place.

4 Using the craft knife, carefully cut the cotton ball in half on a cutting mat to make two half eye-balls. Draw a black pupil on both of them and a few wiggly lines with the red felt pen to make them look bloodshot. Glue them onto the black card and leave to dry.

5 Sellotape one end of the long muslin strip to the back of the bucket and wrap the muslin around the bucket, above and below the eyes, to look like bandages. Thread the end under a strip at the back of the bucket and secure with a knot. Trim the end of the muslin.

6 Take the remaining strip of muslin and cut it in half. Tie each strip to the base of the handle on either side of the bucket.

SCARiLY
SWEET
TREATS

Halloween wouldn't be Halloween without
an abundance of sweet treats and candies.
These ideas for gruesome grub are fun to
make, look truly horrifying, and taste
delicious! There are witch's hat cookies and
sugar rats for the devilishly sweet-toothed
and you can give your guests a fright by
offering them a marzipan beetle or invite
them to delve into the swampy jello. And
who can resist a delicious candy apple?

ghastly ghouls

Create these ghost cupcakes using a marshmallow and a thick meringue frosting that holds its shape but remains soft. Once you've mastered these cupcake versions, why not try making a huge one on a full-size cake?

1 Preheat the oven to 180°C/350°F/gas 4. Line a 15-hole muffin pan with paper cases.

2 Put the flour, salt, and baking powder into a medium bowl, then add the sugar. Add the cubes of softened butter, dotting them evenly into the flour mixture. Blend with an electric mixer, starting on slow speed and working up to medium until evenly incorporated. Add the eggs one at a time, beating to combine.

3 Combine the milk and vanilla extract in a separate jug, and then add to the batter in three parts, beating well each time.

4 Using an ice cream scoop, spoon the batter into the paper cases, filling them three-quarters full. Bake for 15 minutes, or until a toothpick inserted into the center comes out clean. Cool in the muffin pan for a few minutes, then transfer to a wire rack to cool completely before decorating.

5 You will need a small saucepan and a heatproof bowl that will sit neatly on top of it (or use a double boiler, if you have one). Pour a few cups of water into the pan and bring to the boil. The water should not touch the base of the bowl.

6 Whisk the egg whites, sugar, cream of tartar, and salt in the bowl using an electric mixer, then place the bowl above the boiling water and continue whisking until the mixture is hot to the touch and all the sugar has dissolved—about 1–2 minutes.

7 Remove from the heat and, using the mixer on medium-high speed, beat until the eggs form a stiff meringue—about 5 minutes or until hard peaks have formed.

YOU WILL NEED

FOR THE CUPCAKES
* 1⅔ cups (250g) all-purpose (plain) flour, sifted twice
* Pinch of salt
* 2 tsp baking powder
* 1 cup (190g) superfine (caster) sugar
* ½ cup (115g) unsalted butter, at room temperature and cut into cubes
* 2 extra-large (US) or large (UK) eggs, at room temperature
* ½ cup (120ml) full-fat milk
* 2 tsp vanilla extract

TO DECORATE
* 4 extra-large (US) or large (UK) egg whites
* 1 cup (200g) granulated sugar
* ¼ tsp cream of tartar
* Pinch of salt
* 15 white marshmallows (one per cupcake)
* Black fondant or chocolate chips

MAKES 15

8 Secure a marshmallow vertically in the center of each cake using a tiny dab of the meringue, and use a spoon to heap frosting on top of each cupcake to make a ghost shape you like. Smooth the edges with the back of the spoon.

9 Use black fondant or chocolate chips to create "eyes" with a suitably menacing expression.

marzipan **beetles**

To create one of these frighteningly realistic creepy-crawlies, all you need is a little marzipan, some luster dust, and confectioner's glaze. Use pictures of real-life insects as a guide; here, I've made an iridescent jewel beetle. They can be used to decorate cakes or on their own as a creepy appetizer.

YOU WILL NEED

* Confectioner's (icing) sugar, to dust
* 5½oz (150g) marzipan
* Black food coloring
* Luster dust, in whichever colors you choose (see tip)
* Confectioner's glaze (see tip)
* Water or glucose syrup

MAKES 3–4 BEETLES

1 Work on waxed paper and dust your surfaces with confectioner's (icing) sugar to prevent the marzipan sticking. Knead a few drops of black food coloring into a large marble-sized ball of marzipan, making sure the color is evenly distributed.

2 First form the body of your beetle by rolling the marzipan in your hands or on the work surface into an oval pebble shape. Use a scalpel to cut away a little marzipan underneath to give the beetle a steady base.

3 Using a fine paintbrush, brush your beetle with luster dust in the colors you like—use your reference image or make up your own color scheme.

4 Paint on some confectioner's glaze to give a glossy finish. If you wish, you can add extra layers of luster dust and glaze to increase the depth of color and improve the iridescent appearance of the finished beetle.

5 Now use a scalpel or modeling tool to cut in the details on the body—cut a shallow groove to separate the head and the torso, and then shape the eyes

and any other details you want to add. This will reveal the black marzipan under the dust, giving the appearance of the insect's body under sections of the colored shell.

6 Now cut the legs and antlers from a piece of flat marzipan. Carefully attach to the underbelly or face with a little water or glucose syrup and leave to dry on waxed paper overnight.

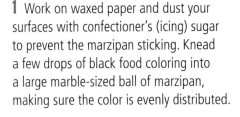

tip

Luster dust is an edible decorating powder. It can be brushed onto other edible decorations, such as chocolate-coated nuts and marzipan, or can be made into a paint using clear alcohol, lemon juice, or clear vanilla extract. Confectioner's glaze is an alcohol-based food-grade shellac solution, which is used for adding shine.

glittery ghosts

These ghost popsickles (lollipops) made from cookie dough are ideal for a Halloween party. Make them in ghoulish white and green and add lots of glitter for some spooky sparkle.

YOU WILL NEED

FOR THE COOKIE POPSICKLES (LOLLIPOPS)
★ 2½ cups (250g) all-purpose (plain) flour
★ 1¼ cups (125g) self-rising (self-raising) flour
★ Pinch of salt
★ 2 sticks (250g) sweet (unsalted) butter, at room temperature
★ ⅔ cup (125g) unrefined superfine (golden caster sugar)
★ 1 egg yolk
★ 1 tsp vanilla extract
★ Ghost cookie cutter
★ 12 popsickle (lollipop) sticks

TO DECORATE
★ 3½ cups (500g) royal icing powder
★ Black or brown food-coloring paste
★ Green food-coloring paste
★ Disposable piping bags with fine and thick tips
★ Edible glitter

MAKES 12

1 First make the cookie dough. Sift the flours and salt into a mixing bowl and set aside. Cream the butter and sugar in another bowl until light and fluffy. Beat in the egg yolk and vanilla extract until they are fully incorporated.

2 Finally, add the flours and mix everything together until all the flour is incorporated and the mixture forms a dough. Put the dough in a sealable food bag and chill for at least 1 hour.

3 Roll your cookie dough so it is about (⅜in./1cm) thick. Cut out 12 cookies using a ghost cutter or template. With one hand, gently twist a popsickle (lollipop) stick into the bottom of each cookie. Place the fingers of your other hand on the top of the cookie so that you can feel where the stick is. Keep twisting the stick until it is at least two-thirds of the way up the cookie.

4 Carefully turn the cookie over. Roll a small sausage of cookie dough and attach it to the bottom of the cookie where the stick is. This will strengthen the cookie and will disappear when it is baked. Place the cookies on a baking sheet lined with waxed (greaseproof) paper and chill for 30 minutes. Meanwhile, preheat the oven to 200°C/400°F/gas 6.

5 Bake for 12–16 minutes until the cookies are golden and smell baked.

6 Prepare the royal icing according to the pack instructions, making it a little thicker than usual as you need it to be thick enough to pipe. Spoon 1–2 tablespoons into a small bowl and tint using the brown or black food-coloring paste. Cover and set aside. Divide the remaining icing into two bowls and tint one of them using the green food-coloring paste.

7 Fit a piping bag with a fine tip and carefully pipe a thin outline around the edge of each cookie. Leave to dry for at least 10 minutes before flooding the middle with more white or green icing, either by using a teaspoon or a piping bag fitted with a thick tip. You may need to thin the icing a little. Leave the icing to dry for half an hour, then outline the cookies again.

8 Put the cookies on some waxed (greaseproof) paper and sprinkle with glitter.

9 Finally, using white icing, pipe a circle for the mouth and 2 ovals for the eyes. Add a dot of black or brown icing to each eye to finish the cookie.

Witches' and wizards' hats

These lovely hats are fun to make with children for Halloween treats or as snacks for budding magicians. They work really well on gingerbread cookies.

YOU WILL NEED

FOR THE COOKIES

* 1 stick (125g) unsalted butter
* ½ cup (100g) dark soft brown sugar
* 2 tbsp water
* 2 tbsp light corn (golden) syrup
* 1 tbsp molasses (treacle)
* 2½ cups (250g) all-purpose (plain) flour
* 1 cup (100g) self-rising (self-raising) flour
* ½ tsp baking soda (bicarbonate of soda)
* 1 tbsp ground ginger
* 2 tsp ground cinnamon
* 2 tsp apple pie spice (mixed spice)
* Finely grated zest (rind) of 1 orange or lemon (optional)
* Witches' and wizards' hat templates on page 119

TO DECORATE

* Confectioner's (icing) sugar, for dusting
* 300g (10oz) rolled fondant (sugarpaste)
* Purple, black, and orange food coloring paste
* 1½ cups (200 g) royal icing powder

MAKES 12

1 First make the cookies. Put the butter, sugar, water, syrup, and molasses in a heavy-based saucepan and melt over a low heat, stirring occasionally. Remove from the heat and leave to cool for a few minutes.

2 Meanwhile, sift the flours, baking soda, and all the spices together into a large bowl, and add the citrus zest (rind).

3 Make a well in the middle of the dry ingredients and pour in the melted mixture. Gently stir in the flour, so that there are no lumps, until the mixture comes together to form a soft dough.

4 Put the dough in a sealable food bag and leave in the refrigerator for at least 1 hour.

5 Roll out the cookie dough and use the templates to cut out the cookies. Place them on a lined baking sheet and chill for 30 minutes. Meanwhile, preheat the oven to 200°C/400°F/gas 6. Bake for 8–12 minutes until the cookies are golden and smell baked.

6 Put 2oz (50g) of the fondant into one bowl and the rest in a second bowl. Tint the smaller portion purple by dipping a toothpick into the coloring paste and applying it to the fondant. Knead until the fondant is evenly colored. Repeat with the larger amount using the black coloring paste.

7 Dust your surface with confectioner's sugar, then roll out the black fondant. Using the templates, cut out six witches' and six wizards' hats and attach them to the cookies. If the icing does not stick, use a little corn syrup or sugar syrup made from dissolving sugar and warm water on a 1:1 ratio, and brush over the cookies.

8 Roll out some purple rolled fondant to ⅛in. (3mm) thick. Cut some thin strips and attach them around the bottom of each witch's hat as a trim.

9 Prepare the royal icing according to the pack instructions. Divide the icing in half and put each portion it its own bowl. Tint one bowl purple and the other orange using food coloring pastes. Fill a piping bag with the orange icing and pipe stars, dots, spiders, and cobwebs on the hats, as well as studs and buckles on the purple trims.

cauldron cake

Fill this chocolate cauldron cake with a selection of spooky candies and maybe a dusting of popping candy for a little extra whizz in your witches' brew.

1 Preheat the oven to 180°C/350°F/gas 4. Grease and base-line two 7-in. (18-cm) cake pans with greased baking parchment.

2 To make the chocolate cake, put the butter and sugar in a mixing bowl and cream until pale and light. Gradually add the eggs and vanilla extract, mixing well between each addition. Melt the semisweet (dark) chocolate in a bowl and stir until smooth. Add the melted chocolate to the cake mixture and combine well.

3 In another bowl, sift together the flour, cocoa powder, baking powder, baking soda (bicarbonate of soda), and salt. Add one-third of the sifted dry ingredients to the cake mixture and mix on low speed until combined, then add one-third of the sour cream. Repeat this process until you have used up all the dry ingredients and sour cream. Add the boiling water and mix until silky smooth. Divide the mixture between the prepared cake pans and bake on the middle shelf of the oven for about 25 minutes or until well risen and a skewer inserted into the middle of the cakes comes out clean. Allow to cool in the cake pan for 3 minutes before transferring to a wire rack until cold.

4 To make the chocolate fudge frosting, melt the chocolate and butter together until smooth and allow to cool. In another bowl, whisk together the milk, sugar and vanilla extract. Stir in the cooled chocolate mixture and beat until smooth and thickened.

5 Place one of the smaller cakes on a serving dish, spread frosting over the top, and lay the larger cake on top. Spread frosting over the top. Using a 4-in. (10-cm) round cookie cutter (or cutting around a plate of that size), stamp out and discard a disc from the middle of the last cake. Place the resulting cake ring on top of the stack of cakes and press gently together. Using a sharp knife, shave off the sides of the cakes so that the edges become rounded and cauldron-shaped.

6 To finish, brush the whole cake with warmed, strained apricot jam and refrigerate for 15 minutes. Cover the whole cake with the remaining frosting, spreading the sides as smoothly as possible. Whip the cream until soft peaks form, then gently fold in some green food coloring paste. Spoon into the top of the cake and scatter the candies (sweets) on top. Arrange the chocolate fingers around the bottom of the cake as firewood.

YOU WILL NEED

FOR THE CAKE
* 7oz (200g) butter, softened
* 1⅔ cups (325g) superfine (caster) sugar
* 4 eggs, lightly beaten
* 1 tsp pure vanilla extract
* 4oz (125g) semisweet (dark) chocolate
* 2⅓ cups (300g) all-purpose (plain) flour
* 2 rounded tbsp unsweetened cocoa powder
* 1 tsp baking powder
* 2 tsp baking soda (bicarbonate of soda)
* Pinch of salt
* 1 cup (225ml) sour cream, at room temperature
* ⅔ cup (175ml) boiling water

FOR CHOCOLATE FUDGE FROSTING
* 8oz (225g) semisweet (dark) chocolate, chopped
* 5oz (150g) butter
* ½ cup (125ml) whole milk
* 2 cups (225g) confectioner's (icing) sugar
* 1 tsp pure vanilla extract

TO FINISH
* 6 tbsp apricot jam
* 1 cup (250ml) heavy (double) cream
* Green food coloring paste
* Assorted candies
* Chocolate-coated finger cookies

SERVES 14–16

swampy jello

Make these on the morning of the party (rather than the day before) and fill with a gruesome combination of confectionery spiders, worms, and teeth. They look particularly good in glass jars, so dig them out if you have some—alternatively just use normal glasses. Any green-colored cordial could be used instead of lime.

YOU WILL NEED

- ★ 6 sheets leaf gelatine
- ★ 3 cups (750ml) lime cordial drink, made according to taste
- ★ Superfine (caster) sugar, to taste
- ★ Green food-coloring paste
- ★ Gummy worms and other creepy Halloween candy (sweets)

MAKES 6-8

1 Soak the leaf gelatine in a dish of cold water for 3 minutes or until softened.

2 Heat half the cordial drink in a pan until just below boiling point, then remove from the heat. Drain the gelatine sheets, squeeze out any excess water, add to the hot juice, and stir until melted. Add the remaining cordial drink and sugar, to taste. Using a toothpick, add a little green food-coloring paste to make the jello a truly slimy color.

3 Allow the jello to cool until it just starts to thicken and is slightly lumpy. Pour the jello into glasses or glass jars and leave until almost set. Push the gummy worms and other creepy Halloween candy (sweets) into the jelly and refrigerate until completely set. Serve with a few extra creepy crawlies on the side.

Look for small, preferably red-skinned apples and red popsicle (lollipop) sticks for these fun and popular candy (toffee) apples. When you come to buy the ingredients for this recipe, why not get some extra apples and at your party, fill a large tub with water, tip in the apples, and play bobbing for apples.

candy apples

YOU WILL NEED

★ 8 small apples

★ 8 popsicle (lollipop) sticks or wooden skewers

★ 1½ cups (300g) superfine (caster) sugar

★ 2 tbsp light corn (golden) syrup

★ Juice of ½ lemon

★ Assorted orange, green, and black sprinkles, for dipping

MAKES 8

1 Wash and thoroughly dry each apple. Carefully push a popsicle (lollipop) stick or wooden skewer into the stalk end of each apple.

2 Put the sugar, syrup, and ⅔ cup (150ml) water in a heavy-based pan over a low heat. Leave until the sugar has completely dissolved.

3 Turn up the heat and simmer until the candy (toffee) turns an amber color. Remove the pan from the heat and carefully add the lemon juice—take care as the hot toffee may splutter.

4 To decorate, quickly dip each apple into the candy (toffee) and swirl it around until evenly coated. Allow to cool for no more than 10 seconds, then dip the bottoms of the apples in the assorted sprinkles. Sit the apples on baking parchment to harden. Serve on the same day.

RUNNING STITCH

Running stitch is probably the simplest hand stitch of all. It is often used to gather a strip of fabric into a ruffle, and also for embroidery.

It is usually worked from right to left, but you can work from left to right if that feels more comfortable. Bring the needle up through the fabric and back down several times, then pull the needle and thread through and repeat, taking care to keep the stitches the same size.

FRENCH KNOT

1 Bring the needle up from the back of the fabric to the front. Wrap the thread two or three times around the tip of the needle.

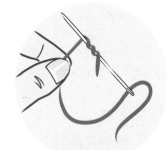

2 Reinsert the needle at the point where it first emerged, holding the wrapped threads with the thumbnail of your non-stitching hand.

3 Pull the needle through to the other side of the fabric.

BACKSTITCH

Work from right to left. Bring the needle up at point A, down at point B, and up again at point C. The distance between A and B should be the same as the distance between A and C. To begin the next stitch, insert the needle at point A again.

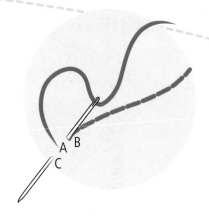

Trimming seams

Once you have sewn two pieces of fabric together, you may need to trim the seam allowancess in order to reduce bulk and help the fabric to lie flat.

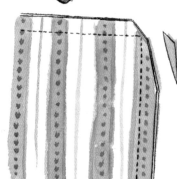

At corners, to achieve neat right angles when the item is turned right side out, simply snip diagonally across the seam allowance, making sure you do not cut through the stitching. Cut small snips in the seam allowances around curved seams to get a neat finish when the garment is turned right side out.

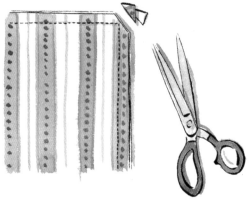

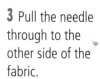

Making an elasticized waistband

Elasticized waistbands are simple to make and are great for children's clothes, as they are easy to put on and take off. The technique can be used for elasticizing cuffs and ankles, too.

1 Turn under the top edge by the width that you would like the waistband to be and stitch in place, leaving a small opening. Topstitching around the top edge as well gives a nice, neat finish.

2 Attach a safety pin to the end of a piece of elastic and thread it through the channel, passing it through the opening in the hem.

3 When the waist is the required size, machine stitch the ends of the elastic together and push them inside the channel. Slipstitch or machine stitch the opening closed.

COSTUME BASICS

Many of the costumes in this book include some basic items that are used in a variety of ways. This section explains how to make them.

Basic top

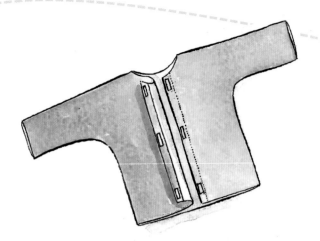

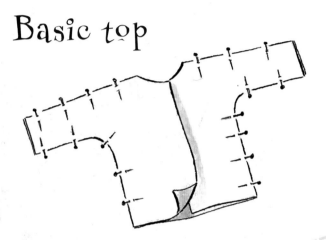

1 Trace and cut out pattern **pieces 26a and 26b** and combine them along the marked lines to make one large pattern. Use this to cut out one front and two back pieces from fabric. With right sides together, pin and stitch the back pieces to the front, along the top of the arms, along the underside of the arms, and down the sides, taking ⅜in. (1cm) seams. Snip into the seam allowances under the arms. Press the seams open.

2 Turn right side out. Turn under ¾in (2cm) on the back edge of both back pieces. Pin and stitch in place near the raw edge. At the center edges of the top, sew the two pieces of a Velcro patch to the underside of one edge and the outside of the other edge, aligning them so that they are at the same distance from the top on both edges. Repeat at the top and bottom using the above diagram as a guide.

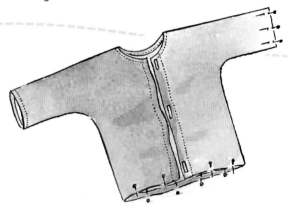

3 Press under ⅜in. (1cm) on the bottom edge, the neck edge, and the lower edges of the sleeves. Pin and stitch these hems in place. Press the top.

Basic pants

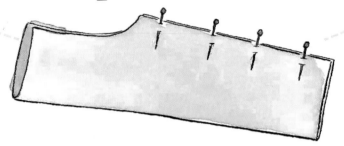

1 Using pattern **piece 27**, cut out two legs from fabric. With right sides together, pin and stitch the long sides of the leg pieces together on both **legs**, taking a ⅜in. (1cm) seam. Press the seam open.

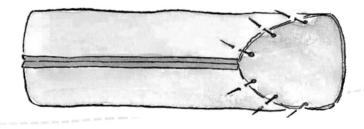

2 Turn one leg **right** side out and slip it inside the other leg. Line up the seams **and** pin and stitch a ⅜in. (1cm) seam around the tops of the legs. It can be a good idea to sew a second line of stitching to reinforce the seam. Make small snips in the seam allowance around the curve, being careful not to cut through the stitches. Turn the pants right side out and press.

3 Press under ¾in. (2cm) at the top edge. Pin and stitch close to the raw edge to make a channel, leaving a small opening in the stitching. Push a piece of elastic through the channel (see page 113 for instructions on how to make an elasticized waistband) and stitch the opening up. Press under ⅜in. (1cm) at the bottom edge of each leg, and pin and stitch these hems in place. Press.

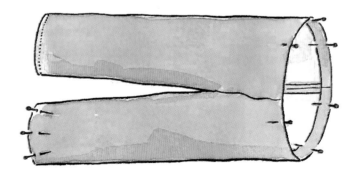

Acknowledgments

Thank you to Louise Turpin for her great design.

Project makers

Emma Hardy: 13-15, 20-21, 22-23, 24-25, 26-27, 28-29, 30-31, 32-33, 34-37, 38-41, 42-45, 46-49, 50-53, 56-59, 60-61, 62-63, 64-65, 66-69, 70-71, 72-73, 74-77, 78-79, 80-83, 84-87
Deborah Schneebeli-Morrell: 16-19
Laura Howard: 10-13
Lily Vanilli: 90-91, 92-93, 94-95, 96-97
Chloe Coker: 98-101
Annie Rigg:102-103, 104-105, 106-107, 108-109

Photography

Debbie Patterson: 8-9, 13-15, 80-87
Heini Schneebeli: **16-19**
Terry Benson: 54-79
Emma Mitchell and Penny Wincer: 10-13
William Lingwood: 89, 102-109
David Munns: 88-97
Martin Norris: 98-101

Illustrations

Michael Hill: 114-117

PATTERN INFORMATION

These patterns are full size, so you do not need to enlarge them. It is best to copy the patt[...]
parchment, or dressmaker's pattern paper and then cut out—that way they can be reused agai[...]
pattern paper or tracing paper is available from sewing stores and online suppliers.) The [...]
you need to follow for the different ages. Each label has a colored background that match[...]
pattern you need to trace. Seam allowances are included where applicable; check the text [...]
seam allowances may vary. Also, check the pattern labeling carefully for special instructio[...]
top (26a and 26b) are in two pieces. You will need to copy both parts and combine them [...]
the patterns before cutting your fabric.

Some of the patterns are shown as halves. When you come to cut out these pieces of fabric[...]
align the CENTER FOLD LINE on the pattern with the fold in the fabric. Where there are l[...]
piece—for example, the left and right front of a shirt—cut one side, then flip the pattern over[...]
and cut the second side.

PATTERN 22
COLLAR FOR BLACK
CAT—*PAGE 72*

PATTERN 23

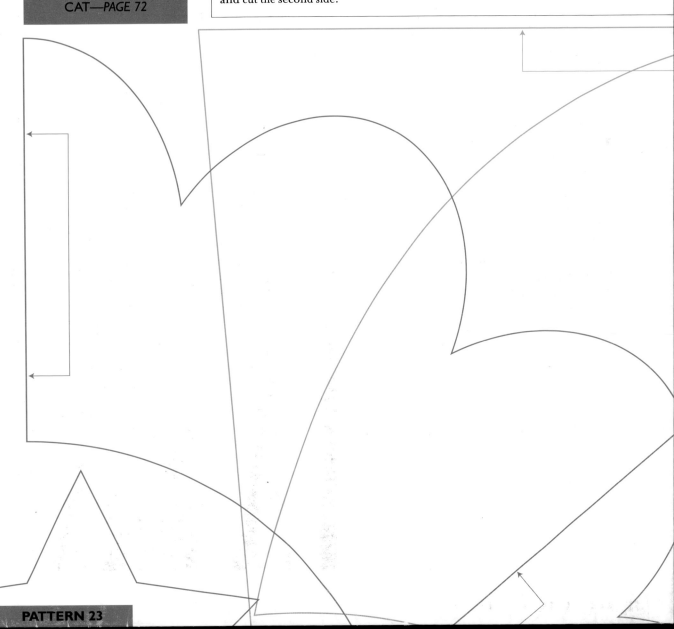

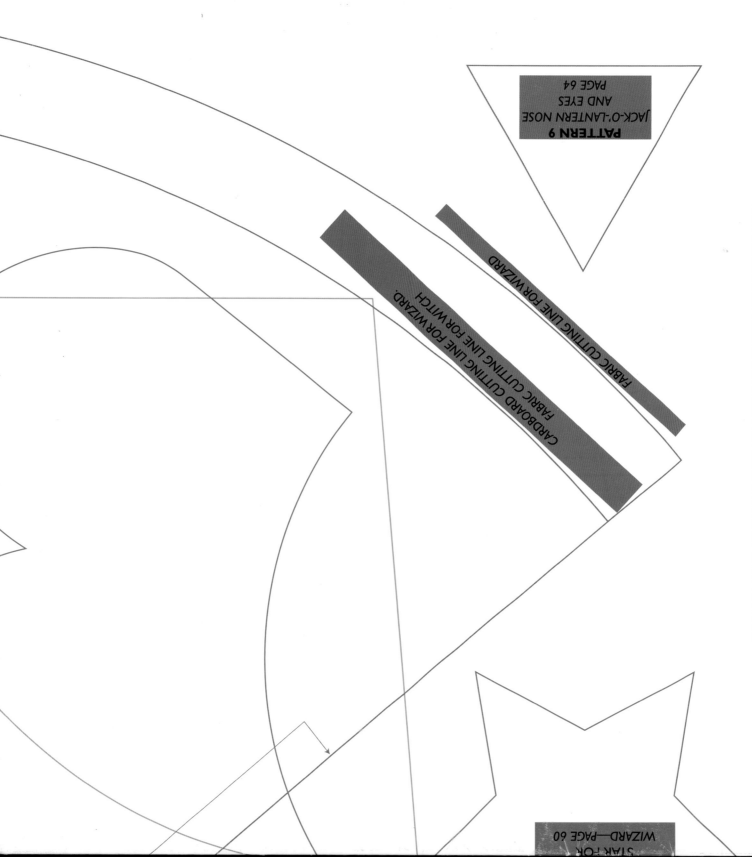

PATTERN 9
JACK-O'-LANTERN NOSE
AND EYES
PAGE 64

FABRIC CUTTING LINE FOR WIZARD

CARDBOARD CUTTING LINE FOR WIZARD
FABRIC CUTTING LINE FOR WITCH

STAR FOR
WIZARD—PAGE 60

TEAR ALONG PERFORATION FOR PATTERNS AND INSTRUCTIONS